Lockdown
AFTERMATH

JOHN R. PISTACCHI

LUMINARE PRESS

WWW.LUMINAREPRESS.COM

Luminare Press
442 Charnelton St.
Eugene, OR 97401
www.luminarepress.com

LCCN: 2021925711
ISBN: 978-1-64388-866-8

I dedicated my first book *Lockdown Capers* to my wonderful spouse (Martha) and loving children, (Ann & Michael).

As much as I love them, I want to dedicate this sequel to my other family, my Parkinson Rock Steady Boxing group and fabulous coach, Michael Reeder.

Their determination to fight off this disease and unwavering friendship and support, has truly been awe inspiring. Plus, they seem to think I'm funny.

READER COMMENTS

Terrific book and project.
Just the medicine I need. –*Bill Walton*

Another good book. Reading some
stories this morning was a great
way to start our day!

Each story brings joy just reading
it and more joy knowing how much
fun you must have writing them.
Thanks for the cheers. Love it

Just rec'd copy of your 2nd book!
Thanks for helping us getting thru these
trying times by writing them. Laughter IS
the best medicine, and I can't wait to
get a good dose of it tonight!

I ordered my depends thru Amazon!
Hopefully they will be here tomorrow
before I read the next chapter.

Thanks for sharing your great
sense of humor!!

Omigosh! You're hysterical! You definitely
need to publish your work! I'm literally
laughing out loud! Soooooo funny!

Your work continues to make me laugh!!!
You are a fabulous writer.

I literally am sitting here with tears rolling
down my face from laughing.

Belly laughing. Will chuckle all day.

Thank you for sharing John.
Great stuff, so funny.

Oh, my goodness John! You're killin me!

Thanks for another great story

What an imaginative storyteller.
So much fun

Thank you for bringing smiles to our
faces and laughter to our lives!

A NOTE FROM THE AUTHOR

As I started writing this sequel to *Lockdown Capers*, it looked like the worst was behind us and life was returning to normal. As time passed, the lockdown was lifted, mandates dropped, and masks started to disappear. With the introduction of vaccines, the infection rates plunged.

Ah, but humans, left to their own devices, are determined to inevitably snatch defeat from the jaws of victory. As I submit this manuscript to the publisher, we are back to record infection rates and a variant is rampaging through our unvaccinated population. Hopefully, by the time the book reaches bookstores, things will have turned around again.

As before, this book is an accumulation of weekly musings shared with my amazingly positive Parkinson Posse and friends. It chronicles the humorous side of Martha and I navigating through our attempts to return to normalcy.

GOOD INTENTIONS

When the Lockdown was announced, we all looked for a positive aspect to having all the time in the world. I decided that this was a unique opportunity to complete all my "in process" projects. I enthusiastically made this list. Boy, I was going to be so productive.

PLANNED ACTIVITIES
UPDATE PASSWORDS
READ NEVER OPENED CAR MANUAL
CHANGE OIL IN CARS
TAKE PHOTOSHOP CLASS
CONSOLIDATE PHOTO ALBUMS
REVIEW INSURANCE POLICIES
OPTIMIZE DISC STORAGE
CANCEL UNUSED CREDIT CARDS
EDIT 2500 + VIDEO CLIPS
WALK 3 MILES PER DAY
LEARN THE GUITAR
LEARN TO MAKE PIZZA FROM SCRATCH
LOSE 10 POUNDS
LEARN SPANISH
LEARN TO MAKE COOKIES FROM SCATCH
REORGANIZE FISHING EQUIPMENT
CLEAN GARAGE
RE-DO REVOCABLE TRUST
START KETO DIET
HANG NEW ARTWORK
PERFECT MAGIC TRICKS
SHARPEN KITCHEN KNIVES
CLEAN OUT FREEZER
RETURN ALL BORROWED TOOLS
READ TWO BOOKS PER WEEK
TAKE UP ASTROLOGY
QUIT WHINING ABOUT LOCKDOWN

One year later, after being released back into the wild, I tallied my actual accomplishments.

PLANNED ACTIVITIES	ACCOMPLISHED
UPDATE PASSWORDS	
READ NEVER OPENED CAR MANUAL	
CHANGE OIL IN CARS	
TAKE PHOTOSHOP CLASS	
CONSOLIDATE PHOTO ALBUMS	
REVIEW INSURANCE POLICIES	
OPTIMIZE DISC STORAGE	
CANCEL UNUSED CREDIT CARDS	
EDIT 2500 + VIDEO CLIPS	
WALK 3 MILES PER DAY	
LEARN THE GUITAR	
LEARN TO MAKE PIZZA FROM SCRATCH	✓
LOSE 10 POUNDS	
LEARN SPANISH	
LEARN TO MAKE COOKIES FROM SCATCH	
REORGANIZE FISHING EQUIPMENT	
CLEAN GARAGE	
RE-DO REVOCABLE TRUST	
START KETO DIET	
HANG NEW ARTWORK	
PERFECT MAGIC TRICKS	
SHARPEN KITCHEN KNIVES	
CLEAN OUT FREEZER	
RETURN ALL BORROWED TOOLS	
READ TWO BOOKS PER WEEK	
TAKE UP ASTROLOGY	
QUIT WHINING ABOUT LOCKDOWN	

MIND GAMES

I am not sure if it is old age, Parkinson's, or being locked up for months, but I am losing the ability to multitask. My short-term memory seems on the wane, and it takes me longer to do any intended task. I will illustrate with a recent attempt to change out a roll of paper towels.

I am in the kitchen and realize that I have not washed my hands in the last ten minutes. In the process of washing them, I use the last paper towel.

No big deal, I will just go to the garage and get another roll. On my way, just as I clear the kitchen island, my laptop dings announcing a new message.

Of course, I must see what that is about immediately.

I head for my office, but by the time I get there, I have no idea why I am standing in the doorway. I look around the room for a hint but get no help.

I go back to the kitchen where the cookies usually hide, but the sight of the empty roll reminds me of my original mission.

I head for the garage but decide that I need to put on my sandals, which are in our hall closet.

By the time I get to the closet, I do not know why I am staring at the shelves.

I decide that I probably needed to replace an ink cartridge. I grab some ink and head back to the office.

Before I replace the ink, the laptop dings again, reminding me that I have not looked at that urgent new message.

It turns out to be a message from my neighborhood watch asking me to keep an eye out for "*Lucky*", the 14th lost neighborhood cat in 24 hours.

John R. Pistacchi

This reminds me to look outside for any Amazon deliveries.

Sure enough, the pencil I ordered earlier this morning has arrived.

I go to the closet to store my new pencil and the sight of my sandals reminds me that I was headed for the garage.

I put on my sandals and almost make it to the garage door when the TV blares that there is BREAKING NEWS.

So, I sit on the couch while Wolf Blitzer tells me the latest emergency, which appears to be the alarming national trend of parents putting their children up for adoption after months of home schooling.

As I am getting up, a tear-jerking commercial begins pleading for donations.

The money is for the care of helpless, starving, abused, and generally pathetic puppies in Outer Mongolia.

I can't stand the heart wrenching images and sad music. I head back to the office to write a check.

As I look out of the office window, I spot a cat walking down the street. *Maybe it's Lucky.*

By the time I reach the front door, the cat is long gone …. but look, another Amazon box!

I go to the kitchen for a knife to open the package.

This reminds me that I should wash my hands after handling the package.

I also remember that I need paper towels.

I once again start for the garage, but as I walk past the couch, I feel tired, and I lay down for a short nap.

I wake up an hour later to Wolf breaking the news that Facebook is no longer running ads for child adoptions.

I go to the kitchen to splash some water on my face and once again conclude that I need some *FX$$$###$$#* paper towels.

OK, this time, nothing will deter me.

I grab an indelible ink sharpie and write "PAPER TOWELS" on my arm.

This is when Martha tells me not to bother because we are completely out of them.

Luckily, she has placed an Insta-cart/Costco order, and some will arrive between midnight and 3:00 AM.

To end the morning on a high note, my smart watch announces that I am way ahead on my step count this morning.

It says that I can therefore take another nap …… which, since I cannot dry my hands until after midnight … I do.

TRAVEL OBSERVATION

PRE-COVID TRAVEL PLANNING KIT

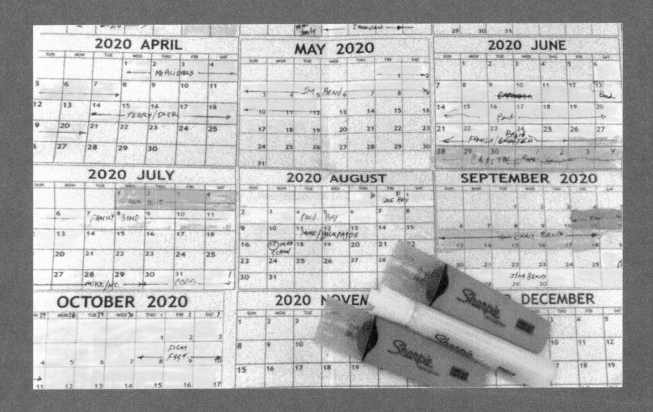

COVID TRAVEL PLANNING KIT

VACCINE MAYHEM

The word is finally out. Vaccines are on their way ... causing untold mayhem and carnage within the cane-waving and walker generation.

There is much confusion out there as to who is eligible. The requirements seem to change on an hourly basis. First responders were for the most part easily identified, herded and vaccinated.

Then, the trouble began.

The first group of seniors had to be over 95 with a permission slip from their parents. Surprised at the amount of unused serum, the authorities immediately changed the rule to anyone over 65. This, too general a description, led to a senior onslaught resulting in massive traffic jams and innumerable walker related crashes and injuries.

So, yesterday, it was back to folks 75 and over but only for essential goat herders (with proof) and pig farmers (with affidavits.)

Now, you would think that California, the State inhabited by the high-tech Masters of data base management (Apple, Google, Oracle....), could come up with a decent, organized distribution system. I mean really! I got a call from my friend Ed who lives in Port Orange, Florida (population 23-30 ... depending on the tide.) He was at his local CVS buying some aspirin when the loudspeaker announced that vaccines were in and if you wanted one, just line up. That easy.

My sister-in-law and her friends formed a vaccine posse. They then split up and drove around Bend, Oregon until one heard of an open distribution center. With walker tires burning rubber, they stormed the place Jan. 6 style. They got vaccinated.

A distant acquaintance in Boise was stopped in front of his local CVS. A nurse jumped in the car and vaccinated him before the light changed. *(I must admit that this one is more of a rumor.)*

Then, to add insult to injury, a number of our local friends smugly called us to inform us that they got *their* vaccine. "Neener, Neener!". They decided to ignore the very specific rules about age and qualifications and showed up at the Petco Park mega vaccine center .... They were vaccinated, no questions asked.

The distribution channels were also a complete mess, making it impossible to

John R. Pistacchi

decipher who had refrigerators able to store the magic potion.

To relieve some tension, I went for a walk. That is when I heard a distant jingle. I recognized the tune immediately and chased down our local ice cream truck. Unfortunately, they were fresh out. *Grrrrr... so close.*

Meanwhile, we were getting so many calls from friends being vaccinated that our answering machine exploded.

OK, now it's getting personal and ***it is on***. Time for Warp Speed action. We fire up every electronic device in the house enabling us to monitor 12 web sites simultaneously, 24/7.

Finally, at 2:00 AM, one of the computers chirps cheerfully and announces that the University of California San Diego (UCSD) is once again sticking seniors 65 and over.

By 4:30 AM, we each have an appointment for early next week … so far so good.

It still concerns me that the website has not taken down the statement requiring a valid goat herder license, but we conclude that it is just an oversight.

We're going in, we're storming the ramparts!

STORMING THE RAMPARTS

OK, where were we?

Ah yes, Martha and I had our appointments to get vaccinated. They were 4 hours apart. We figured that showing up together early and being such a cute couple, would melt some hearts and qualify us to get pierced at the same time.

I am fretting over the prominent goat herder requirement still posted on the website. I could kick myself for letting my herding license expire last year... but who knew?

So, with the remote possibility of getting busted, we devise a backup plan. Martha will be my caretaker (she really is, but we don't have notarized proof). I therefore implore her to put on her Halloween sexy nurse outfit.

For my part, I need to look as pathetic as the abused puppies on TV commercials. I skip my morning dose of dopamine (anti-tremor drug) and eat 12 candy bars on the way to the center. This ensures that I will be in a shaky, sugar induced coma by our appointment time. Fool-proof plan.

We are now in line with what must be 1000 cars full of geezers like ourselves all rolling up their sleeves. It has the feel of a parking lot at an RV and Hawaiian timeshare sales convention.

Then, as we start to relax, we spot a uniformed officer walking toward us with a clipboard. It is a woman. This probably negates one of the intended effects of Martha's uniform.

She stops at the car in front of us and before we know it, the 90 something driver is out of the car with his hands on the hood being frisked for proof of something.

After examining his driver's license, passport, and dentures, she puts a small blue sheet of paper behind his wind shield wiper and motions for him to move forward.

We are next in line and by now, I don't even have to fake my condition. The officer asks how old we are. I announce like a child that I am ***74 and a third***. She shakes her head and informs us that the rules changed 1/2 hour ago back to 75 and above, with no exceptions. Martha explains our plight and that every one of our friends has been vaccinated and won't play with us until we get our shots.

NOTHING, NOT EVEN A SMILE.

Remembering the goat herder angle, I dig in my wallet and pull-out old pictures of me and our young children at a petting zoo herding baby goats (I brought the photos as a backup to our backup plan .... *Fast Johnny always thinking ahead.*)

NOTHING DOING. She demands our licenses and disappears to consult with the head vaccine commander.

Finally, she comes back, tells us that our appointments have been officially canceled and *"no-go kids, strict enforcement today".* I am suddenly worried that we have been placed on a vaccine blacklist.

With that, she drapes across our windshield a humongous bright yellow banner featuring an enormous black **X** visible from the Hubble telescope. Now, with our Scarlet Letter firmly attached to our car, we are escorted to the line of shame.

This line is reserved for bad seniors. We are left there roasting in the sun as an example to other potential senior banditos.

We sit there, avoiding eye contact with the cars parading by in the lane next to us. These cars are packed with honking, laughing, cheering and perhaps drunk vaccinated seniors. That's when we spot Sally and Marvin, a neighborhood couple in their 50's who for some unknown reason have made it their mission to terrorize local seniors. They race through the neighborhood like they are in the Indy 500 and Marvin is always yelling at meandering seniors to get off his lawn.

But here they are. Their kids are hanging out of the window waving their blue sign yelling "LOSERS" at the stalled folks in the banished lane. This is when Marvin flips us off and peals rubber toward the exit. Oh well, someday, they will be old and learn about the "Golden Days", or is it years? I can't remember.

Finally, a gate opens and the shame parade is allowed to slowly move out of PETCO Park (with mandatory lights on ... funeral style). We are **Not** deterred however, and decide to double down.

Back at home, after buying 6 more laptops (enabling us to now monitor 67 websites), Martha has managed to get us two dozen appointments, all the way into June. We may end up getting our shots in Mendocino, but as our daughter says, "What else do you two have to do?"

With that out of the way, we start plotting our next backup plan. We are going in as CVS essential workers. All we need is a few more 40-foot register receipts to look legitimate.

TRUTH ALERT: Our ejection from Petco Park is absolutely true, as is the yellow sign and lane of shame. The rest may be somewhat embellished. I am not sure how much though, as I have still not come down from my sugar high.

STORMY WEATHER

We, once again, found ourselves with reservations at Petco Park for 8:30 AM.

With confidence, we reviewed our checklist:

1. Driver's license...check

2. Printed Appointment bar code... check

3. Email copy of appointment...check

4. Phone version of bar code...check

5. Short sleeve shirt...check

6. Water bottle...check

7. Emergency backup novel...check

8. Overnight bag...check

9. CVS receipts...check

We are finally off. It seems a little windy and we comment on white caps dominating the San Diego Bay. We observe surf breaking on the pedestrian walkway. *Hmmm*, never seen that before.

We should have picked up on potential problems when the first set of medical tents flew out of the stadium in a Blue Angels formation. The second hint was the tumbleweed and small cat rolling past our car.

After an hour in line, we get to the gate. We are informed by a very nice security guard that a 100-year windstorm has reached our shores. The ferocity of the storm is resulting in a shortage of tents. *PETCO PARK is now closed*. We can come back anytime during the next 2 days, no questions asked. (While she is talking to us, a second wave of tents takes flight along with a petite nurse.)

So, before we take flight ourselves in Martha's very light car, we head for home.

As soon as we walk through the door, a friend calls to inform us that our VONS grocery store has somewhat short lines and is vaccinating people.

We put our rain gear back on and off we go in the direction of our local VONS. Within 10 blocks of our destination, we find ourselves behind a massive line of cars. This, we conclude is the line for vaccinations. We turn off the engine and read our novels until the line starts moving. One hour and twenty minutes later, we pull up to a tent. A gentleman asks us to open our trunk. OK, this is new (and a little weird). He then proceeds to place a 30-pound box of food in the trunk telling us to thank God for today's bounty. That is when we discover that we have been in a Rock Church food distribution line.

After returning the box of food (minus a banana) and a cash donation, we continue to the grocery store .... who's next available appointment by now is sometime in the year 2023.

SWEET SUCCESS

For the third time, we have reservations at PETCO PARK for 8:30 AM.

I am writing this real-time to accurately describe this event. It appears that some readers are starting to think that I am being a little loose with the facts by the time I write late at night. It might just be the effect of my Shirley Temple nightcaps.

Anyway, we're pretty sure today's the day.

The wind seems to be down with gusts not strong enough to airlift medical tents and rain them down on the parking lot like Operation Desert Storm era SCUD missiles.

Also, our investment in additional hardware for our mega high tech reservation war room has paid off.

We have appointments every 15 minutes until Petco Park closes, or all the tents blow down again. A few late afternoon appointments are in Seattle and Tucson, but we will be really close to the airport and have plenty of unused miles.

We have scoured our local news and the web for any signs of impending tornados and flash floods. We also investigated the top ranked plagues that could possibly preempt our effort. Let's see:

1. Boiling frogs ... no sign of those (or locusts).

2. Pestilence of livestock ... all neighborhood pets seemed OK.

3. Thunderstorms, hail, and darkness .... OK, that was Monday and Tuesday and not predicted back until the weekend.

Getting our shots today would also eliminate the unresolved issue we stayed up late last night discussing. The dilemma is this: What if only one of us could get vaccinated? I mean, the grandkids like my pizza, but they *LOVE* their Nana. Martha turned the tide in her favor a few years ago after attending a seminar entitled *"1000 ways to spoil and bribe your Grandchildren to buy their love"*. But, I totally digress.

OK, so it does seem like a go. We check our prep list once again:

1. 2 forms of ID ... check

2. 3 electronic versions of bar code...... check

3. Dozen candy bars…...check

4. Sexy nurse outfit (with wig added so no one recognizes Martha).

5. Photos of petting zoo goats … check

6. Overnight bag …. Still in car.

7. CVS receipts

With that, we are off. We get behind the long line (that we are now very familiar with).

The streets are jammed in every direction as thousands of seniors want to get vaccinated or have forgotten that the San Diego Chargers are now in Los Angeles.

There is such a huge crowd that I ask Martha to verify that it really is vaccination day and not the day that PETCO gives away bacon wrapped chew sticks. No, she is sure and points to all the tents and rolled up sleeves. I then look around one last time for food distribution trucks in the area *... Fool me once.*

We arrive at the first checkpoint, provide our ID cards and the attending nurse begins to type. I get nervous as she is typing way more than seems necessary.

She glances up occasionally, smirks, takes a deep breath, then starts typing again. Then, while keeping an eye on us, she whispers something into her wrist radio.

We now spot the uniformed attendant from our last visit heading in our direction. OK, I am now totally freaking out. This is it; *we are going to vaccine jail!*

I tell Martha to adjust the wig and *be ready to run*. I tell her to not look back and just save herself. As she is reaching slowly for the door handle, the nurse with a smile says we are in.

She pleasantly hands us vaccination cards and apologizes for the delay …. She explains that it took quite a while to cancel our other 512 appointments. It seems that we forgot to power down our reservation search engines before leaving the house and they have been very busy.

The rest of the story is dull. We were given painless shots, waited our 15 minutes to check for side effects, got our second shots scheduled for late February and were home by 9:30 AM.

Oh, I almost forgot one final embarrassing moment. We were passing the stalled line of bad seniors. Suddenly,

Martha snaps and, completely out of character, sticks her head out of the window and while waving our vaccination cards starts yelling, "Neener Neener."

Good thing this is over. I think the pressure might have been getting to her.

Our wonderful, amazingly concerned, and supportive children can also finally relax and maybe stop calling us every 5 minutes to see if we were vaccinated yet.

TRUTH ALERT: In case you have concluded that we have been shamelessly abusing the system and wrongfully hoarding appointments, let me clear the air. Our reservation super center is a figment of my warped imagination (We own one laptop) as is the number of appointments made.

BOOSTER BLUES

As you recall, after several failed attempts and managing to avoid vaccine jail, we finally got our first shot. It was now time to prepare for the dreaded booster.

We were somewhat apprehensive due to the high number of friends warning us of negative effects from this 2nd shot.

In addition to warnings, we received much unsolicited and frankly sometimes questionable advice. A minor list follows:

Pre-Shot Advice:

- Do not take Advil for a few days before.

- Take lots of Advil to get ahead of the migraine headed your way.

- Avoid Advil, take Tylenol.

- Tylenol is a rebranded Chinese memory altering drug. Stick to Aspirin.

- Drink lots of water.

- Do not drink any water. Your bloat will dilute the effect of the drug.

- Eat plenty because you will not feel like eating for weeks.

- Fast for 12 days prior to appointment.

- The 2nd shot either makes you infertile or turns you into a rabbit.

- "Will make you strong Like Bull" (from Russian refugee cutting in line).

Post-Shot Advice:

All comments fell somewhere between the two below:

Friend #1 …. No problem whatsoever, a piece of cake. I chopped wood for the fireplace, did a Costco run and climbed Mt. Whitney over the weekend.

Friend # 2…... OMG, in bed for 2 days shaking like a leaf with epic headache, 125-degree fever, being fed from a tube and unable to move. Not enough strength to dial 911.

Martha decided that there were just too many conflicting variables to allow a credible preparation plan. She chose to fight whatever came her way with strength.

She thus started on a push up and plank Pilates program.

I, on the other hand, (a major male wuss who goes down for the count at the first hint of a sniffle), need to nest and prepare for the worst.

I call dibs on "NAPPY" couch …. so named because no one can lay on it and not be asleep within 3 minutes. ***See Note #1***

Now, I go over my ***booster shot*** list…

- Comfortable couch … check
- Warm blanket …. check
- Hot water bottle …check
- Cold packs …. check
- Cell phone with 911 on speed dial …. check
- Soft pillow ….check
- Candy bars ………………check
- Robe & slippers………...check
- Advil………check
- Tylenol…… check
- Aleve … check

- Aspirin ……… check
- Olive oil …. check
- Goat milk …... check
- Small bottle of fresh South African crocodile tears … check
- Malloque instructions ……….check ……... ***See Note #2***

NOTE #1: We have dozens of photos of our unsuspecting house guests in comical (i.e., drooling) positions. We keep these in our lock box at the bank for potential blackmail purposes.

NOTE #2: Malloque …. My Italian grandmother's method of curing headaches by warding off the devil. This involves a bowl of hot water into which you introduce 3 drops of high-quality super extra virgin olive oil while repeating "be gone devil" (in Italian, while rubbing your forehead in a circular motion). If the oil drops scatter, the devil has skedaddled along with your headache. If the drops stick together, you my friend are in deep S***! Your only hope is repeating the procedure using freshly squeezed goats' milk instead of water and South African crocodile tears instead of oil.

Even though Petco Park was up and down like a yo-yo all week, none of our "MY CHART" UCSD medical bulletins canceled our appointment. I think they blared fake bulletins to further thin the herd via heart attacks.

So, except for being overly confident, not using our GPS and getting lost in downtown San Diego (having driven to Petco Park at least 4 times in the recent past), all went well.

We were back home by 10:30 AM.

At noon, we had a sandwich but found ourselves uncharacteristically adding potato chips, avocado dip and Cheetos to the menu.

I felt extremely fatigued and laid on Nappy couch. Within my allotted 3 couch minutes, I fell into a Moderna induced coma resulting in snoring worthy of the San Diego Zoo Roar and Snore program. (This according to Martha who I believe greatly exaggerates my snoring volume …. After all, *I have **never** heard myself snore.*)

At 2:00 PM I am startled awake by Martha frantically yanking on my sleeve. She wants me to wake up, get up, and immediately make her a pizza. I recall that I saved enough pizza dough last week to make an emergency backup personal pie that, suddenly, I start craving as well.

So, by 2:30 PM, we are feasting on pizza while looking around for dessert.

When we break into the left-over Halloween candy, we realize that we are reacting to the shot in a way absolutely no one mentioned as a possibility.

A distant college memory bubbles up to the surface and identifies our condition.

No doubt about it,

WE HAVE THE MUNCHIES!

BY 9:00 PM we have consumed:

- 2 village size bags of Cheetos
- 3 bags of Doritos
- 12 cups of popcorn
- 4 ice cream cones
- Miscellaneous meat products
- 12 chocolate pudding cups

That is when Martha calls it quits.

She is developing a headache, wobbles upstairs and falls into the Moderna coma. (I record her epic snoring on my iPhone for potential later use. I will place the recording in our lock box.)

At 10:00 PM, I check Martha's pulse. She is not only in a Moderna comma, but now her arm hurts and she is running a 103-degree fever. This trifecta results in immobilizing her completely. I would have stuck around to comfort her but there really was not much I could do. Besides, I spotted a king-size Snicker bar in the pantry.

At 11:00 PM, the doorbell rings as I am fixing myself a prosciutto and meatball sub. It's either Domino's delivering my family size pizzas or McDonald's bringing me my egg McMuffins and chicken McNuggets.

By 12:30, I also have a massive migraine but inexplicably turn into John Travolta singing *"I've got chills …. their multiplying and …... I'm losing control"* from *Grease*. Good thing Martha got rid of my bell bottoms a few weeks ago.

The refrigerator is now empty except for some useless broccoli and asparagus bags …. which, incredibly, tempt me for a nanosecond.

That is when I go to bed to not stir for 12 hours (next to my lovely and petite freight train level snoring princess bride.)

Except for massive fatigue, sore arms, intermittent headaches, and occasional comas, we manage to survive the next couple of days and reluctantly return to our normal diet.

So, good luck with your 2nd shot and …

Beware of the munchies effect!

TATER TOTS

We are starting to assume that things will get back to normal within months instead of the years for which we were preparing.

It is therefore time to review some of our major early decisions and adjust accordingly.

Very early on, we decided that we would not hoard, well at least not in the traditional sense (i.e., cleaning out a shelf of toilet paper in a grocery store).

No, we would be discreet non-hoarding citizens.

We started getting hourly bulletins on our smart watches warning us of massive hoarding. We also noticed that Instacart was now taking up to 2 weeks to deliver our chocolate covered Bon Bons. Needless to say, we got a little concerned. So, just in case, we bought an emergency backup 10-foot industrial size freezer.

We snuck it into the garage in the middle of the night so as to not arouse suspicion from the neighbors. We draped it with a boat cover and attached a couple of oars to make it look less conspicuous.

Our non-hoarding ruse was very simple: We would simply buy two of everything each time we dared enter a store.

In case of a store interrogation, we had our story down: We were also shopping for my bed ridden sister-in-law.

The last part of our non-hoarding plan was to never actually use anything from the freezer. The contents would be strictly for dire emergencies.

Eventually, with our DE-LUXE industrial model "SEAL A MEAL" working 24/7, we filled our 2-ton capacity freezer with the essentials of life.

When it took both of us and an Amazon driver sitting on the freezer to close the latch, we decided "NO MAS". We would now live off the bounty Instacart and Door Dash could deliver and fit in our regular refrigerator.

The months slipped by. We have not opened the freezer since approximately the announcement that all who wanted a COVID test could get one ... hahaha, the good old days of government levity.

We are thinking it might be time to use up some of our frozen bounty. Also, we are curious about expiration dates (which were not going to be of concern if faced with starvation.)

There is also the nagging thought that if we had a power failure, we might need to remortgage our house to replace the food.

We are actually very excited and curious as to what we stashed and once considered essential foods.

After all, Martha is a green and veggie person, whereas I have more of a meatball sandwich and ice cream personality, potato-potado.

However, we were both perplexed when our first look into the abyss yielded four huge bags of Tater Tots. Not any size bags, but Costco Paul Bunyan community size bags.

We know that Tater Tots were a thing in the 60's but they seemed to have disappeared along with bell bottom pants and

disco. We have not eaten a Tater Tot since a memorable breakfast in San Francisco in early 1962 when they were actually a featured dish.

I accused Martha of falling for VON'S trick of "buy 1 get 3 free" for products they can't get rid of. She points out that she is not strong enough to lift that many Tater Tot bags into a cart (a fact).

Then, she accuses me of instacarting while under the influence. She has become a firm enforcer of the rule "*Don't Drink and Prime*" after a few Christmas shopping mishaps of her own.

I also refuse to believe that my Shirley Temples have anything to do with this abundance of frozen taters.

At a stalemate, we decide that it really does not matter how they got into the freezer, they are there. We also need to act quickly as the the expiration date is rapidly approaching.

We try to dump them on the Rock Church for distribution, but the pastor runs us off.

He tells us that his flock has more pride than that and have we no shame.

(He is still mad at us for causing trouble in the food distribution line last week.)

He suggests that we come back when we have *real* potato-based products, like French fries. He is also miffed at our attempt to pawn off goods about to expire.

We therefore face our only remaining solution and come up with a menu for the next 3 months:

- Monday ... Shrimp and Tater Tots

- Tuesday ... Chicken and Tater Tots

- Wednesday ... Pork Roast and Tater Tots

- Thursday ... Big Salad and Tater Tots

- Friday .... Fish and Tater Tots

- Saturday ...... Pasta and Tater Tots

- Sunday...... *Tater Tots with a side of Tater Tots*.

With the Tater Tots crisis resolved, we get back to our original goal: to evaluate what is in the freezer. Under the bags of taters, we discover another Paul Bunyan size bag. This time it's 20 pounds of already cooked, but frozen, *Won Tons*. Oh Lord!

WON TONS

As you recall, peering into our emergency backup freezer yielded a cornucopia of Tater Tots and a S### Load of wontons.

We dealt with the taters, but the Won Tons were a bigger surprise and problem. After-all, we did have a vague and distant memory of frying taters at home before the invention of the oven.

We, however, have absolutely no recollection of eating a Won Ton outside of an Asian restaurant since…... well, like **_ever_**. So, here we are again with extra food about to expire and the need to dispose of it.

Donating food to the Rock Church was out of the question after being served a restraining order from the pastor.

We put our heads together, got creative and hatched a new improved fool proof plan.

We visited my 99-year-old Italian Aunt Sophie at the memory care center. Her nearsightedness and memory lapses enabled us to easily convince her that we brought her a new kind of cannelloni.

She and her Italian Club, pot smoking, poker buddies (all nearsighted) went through the 20-pound bag of Won Tons in less than a week … _Mission accomplished!_

Unfortunately (and somehow unforeseen), the "mile-high club" over here had now become addicted to their new munchie treat.

The Girls became desperate and greatly agitated when the kitchen manager refused to add soy sauce covered cannelloni to the daily menu.

The next day, they grabbed their _"Don't Tread on Me"_ face masks, hijacked the facility service van and careened out of the campus in the general direction of Little Italy.

The hot uniformed 87-year-old campus cop ("The Kid"), gave chase but his 3-wheel, 2 speed scooter was no match for the floored, tire squealing, rubber burning van charging the gate.

He was left behind blinded and coughing in a cloud of dust smelling of burnt rubber and a mixture of *Vic's VapoRub and Ben Gay.*

Ignoring the Amber Alert now blaring over the radio, they gingerly exited the van.

This is when all hell broke loose.

With canes waving menacingly, they stormed the Mona Lisa Italian Delicatessen demanding that they stock up on the fancy new cannelloni pasta.

After bailing them out and receiving a restraining order from Mona Lisa's, we went home to rethink our approaches to our excess food issues.

We realized, that at this rate of restraining orders, we would have nowhere to go when the "stay at home" order finally got lifted.

But, boy, I have massively digressed again.

OK, back to the original task of uncovering the contents of this gargantuan freezer.

Since it is not a side by side, we have no idea of the contents except on a layer-by-layer basis.

Unfortunately, there were a few power failures during the past 9 months.

Fortunately, these interruptions were not long enough to melt the amount of ice necessary to cause a major overflow resulting in Won Tons and frozen steaks floating down our street and into our neighbor's homes *(as happened during the 1998 county blackout.... Ref. San Diego County Neighborhood Vs. Pistacchi).*

However, enough ice did melt and refreeze to turn the entire remaining freezer contents into a massive frozen solid popsicle.

It is obvious that we are no longer in control and have no choice. We must go into full blown archeology excavation mode.

CAUTIONARY TALES

DO NOT DRINK AND PRIME!

I was sitting in my living room having my second Shirley Temple nightcap when it hit me:

I was almost out of the sugar substitute "Stevia". I immediately jumped on Amazon to order some. I don't even know what the inside of a store looks like anymore, my only contact with products being through Amazon. Sure enough, the site carries Stevia. Then, I discover that I can get 1000 packets for only $3.00 more than the 100 packets package, which is only $2.00 more than the 50-count box, which is only $2.50 more than a single packet out of an open box.

My next day delivery:

Like I said, don't drink and Prime!

ALSO, BEWARE OF FALSE ADVERTIZING!

Advertised steak

Delivered steak

THE BIG DIG (PART I)

OK, where were we?

Ah yes, our attack on the Covid anti-starvation survival freezer.

After analyzing our Tater Tot and Won Ton debacles, we decide that one giant bag of frozen booty at the time is just not going to cut it.

I truly believe that we are only one restraining order away from our children finding a facility with many care levels but featuring a high voltage fence.

It seems like we absolutely need to empty this monster by excavating the entire content. Only then, can we truly visualize the magnitude of our dilemma and devise a more cohesive plan of action.

After finding the proper excavation gear and outfits on Amazon, (costing twice as much as the food we are struggling to save), obtaining a permit from the city, and ensuring that the Rock Church restraining order perimeter does not include our garage, we are ready to dive into our frozen zoo.

However, we have second thoughts. So, while our outfits are still returnable and refundable, we decide to try one more gambit …… a sort of "Hail Mary" pass.

This is one that our kids used with amazing success throughout college while moving from one place to another.

Unfortunately, there is no way that Martha and I can pull this off by ourselves. For this effort to succeed, we need some serious manual labor type of help and possibly an industrial strength forklift.

It used to be impossible to get instant help, any kind of help, on short notice for a small job.

You had to peruse the Yellow Pages and make dozens of unanswered calls. Eventually, and long after you forgot why you needed help, a guy in a no sleeve T-Shirt would show up at your door asking, "YOU GOT A PROBLEM?"

There was no help around whatsoever. Our streets were deserted once the children were dropped off at school. The only movement and excitement might come from the occasional tumble weed rolling down the sidewalk (sometimes large enough to set off a car alarm).

Well, things have sure changed and if you ask me, for the better. Especially for what do they call us? The most vulnerable among us?

Now, bodies are everywhere. Amazon drivers litter our streets. They scurry from house to house like deranged mice looking for cheese. If you throw in trucks from Fed Ex, UPS, USPS, DHL and various lost private delivery trucks, you can easily have 10 strong and husky men and women roaming your block looking down at iPads.

With packages blocking their view, they can be as entertaining as bumper cars at the County Fair .... but a little scary at sundown when it turns into the night of the living dead out there.

John, you are driving me crazy, where are you going with this?????

Patience my little butterflies.

By now, there are 2-4 drivers within reach. This is where my enormous Northern California Salmon net comes into play. After netting huge wily salmon on Monterey Bay for years, these kids are not even a challenge. They can be netted like a ball of unsuspecting anchovies.

After a successful driver scoop, one of two things will happen. If the driver stops flailing, you can calmly negotiate a release in return for a few hours of labor.

If, however, your catch manages to escape the net and comes at you yelling, you immediately sit on the curb. You instantly turn into the feeble citizen you are supposed to be with Parkinson's and dementia. It does not hurt to drool a little as you begin babbling incoherently.

You apologize for your behavior but claim that you have never quite recovered from that awful salmon incident at sea and you now see salmon everywhere. Then, keep babbling.

I guarantee that the driver will sit next to you, put an arm around you and beg to help you in any way possible.

And voila, same day help!!!

I am not sure that I should continue to divulge this knowledge. At a party last year, after a few too many Shirley Temples, I spilled the beans. The following week, Big 5 reported a shortage of large nets resulting from a spike in senior shop lifting incidents. Then, the neighborhood police radios started blowing up with reports of drivers abandoning their trucks and being chased by net waving seniors.

OMG, I have so digressed. Back to our gambit.

At midnight, we met up with Alphonso and Gidget (two Amazon drivers we managed to subdue earlier in the day). Luckily, one of them had commandeered a full-size forklift from the local Amazon warehouse.

They helped us maneuver the freezer onto the lift and we were off. We dropped the unit off in a darkened corner of the 975-acre Rock Church parking lot. Then, we placed an enormous "FREE" banner across the top. After wiping the thing down to eliminate any fingerprints and with our pandemic masks still in place, we peeled forklift tire rubber out of there. Our two hostages were driving while Martha and I were hanging on to the side rails doing high fives. The perfect crime.

.... Well, except for one minor detail.

We forgot about the security cameras that our HOA installed throughout the area to keep an eye on feeble, unruly, and rambunctious elders like ourselves.

As we open the garage door the next morning, we discover our freezer in the driveway with two notes replacing our banner.

One is banning us from the HOA and demanding our presence at the next Board meeting to discuss our possible arraignment.

The other is from the pastor demanding our presence at a hearing to discuss our excommunication.

Oh Lord, please don't let our kids hear about this.

Anyway, we are now back to ground zero, facing our inevitable excavation.

Early on, we decided to divide the freezer in two sections. Each of us would have 1/2 of the freezer (a his and hers section). We taped the areas off like our kids did when sharing a bedroom. We assumed that all of the packages would respect the established boundaries making it simple to find our respective parcels.

We decided to take turns excavating and discovering our long-forgotten acquisitions. We also agreed that, to save our marriage, no matter what surfaced, the party not responsible for the ridiculous item uncovered would be limited to one eye roll and **no sarcastic comments whatsoever**.

Of course, this is when we remember that the unit had been without power since the night of our little forklift caper. I immediately notice that my half-thawed meatballs have floated over to Martha's side while some loose asparagus has meandered over to hug one of my chicken breasts.

But, refusing to be deterred by anything anymore, we take our first swing of our brand new $75.00 pickax.

We dig a trench from the top of the freezer to the bottom. This somewhat defines our separate areas of digging.

Our first extraction comes from Martha's side: Enough broccoli bags to build a Rockefeller Plaza size Christmas tree.

Martha immediately gives me *"THE LOOK"* and I settle for one very discreet eye roll.

THE BIG DIG (PART II)

Before we dive into our final excavation, I want to share some breaking news on our issues with the HOA and the Rock Church.

I am pleased to announce that the HOA not only dropped all charges but offered me the presidency of the association. This sudden reversal of attitude occurred shortly after we produced photographs (retrieved from our lock box) of an informal board meeting at Ocean Beach involving the use of illegal substances and recorded negative comments disparaging meandering seniors living in the area.

That only left the Pastor to deal with.

We went back to our (so far) magical play book and performed a deep search of our lock box. Amazingly, we came up empty. I mean *Butkus, NADA*. Not even a recording of a parishioner singing off key or yawning during service. In a last dich effort, I bought some night vision goggles and stalked the church campus. Unfortunately, I was unable to complete my mission. I was chased out of there by the two night watchmen after a parishioner reported a pervert with binoculars near the kiddy swings. Good thing the guards were overweight, and that Johnny is still pretty fast. However,

if they had caught me, I was totally prepared to go into my mumbling feeble elder with Parkinson's and dementia routine that works so well with Amazon drivers. I bet they would have even escorted me home.

However, due to this monumental undercover failure, we are facing the excommunication committee with absolutely zero leverage.

Fortunately, at the last minute, a plausible technicality was discovered. Not belonging to the congregation posed a slight problem that would result in a nightmarish amount of paperwork requiring us to join the Church in order to be kicked out.

Fortunately, cooler heads prevailed.

We negotiated a settlement. We were fully exonerated (through clenched teeth) but our restraining order was extended to a 2-mile radius and now required an armed guard to be posted 24/7 in front of our garage until the freezer was empty.

OK, finally back to this #@##@##@# endless freezer story.

As I have previously documented, Martha and I have very different tastes in food.

Martha is more of a veggie fan, leading her to be *petite* (French for petite).

I, on the other hand, am more of a pasta of any kind type leading me to be *"big boned,"* (Italian for chubby).

For most of my life, nothing green (except avocados) passed my lips. I can't tell you how relieved and elated I was to learn later in life that avocados were classified as a fruit!

I can probably illustrate our differences better via dessert choices:

Big Boned

Petite

In an abundance of caution, we left the unit plugged in for a week to refreeze the contents and avoid floating debris. Unfortunately, this also resulted in our having to "borrow" an Ace Hardware driver to help us with the industrial size crowbar and blow torch required to open the frozen solid lid.

We have noticed that It is getting much harder to get same day help again. I have no one to blame but myself. (Damn Shirley Temples and my big mouth.)

We must be more careful. The drivers are on to the net waving seniors. They are leerier and ferret-like skittish.

Most now carry Mace sprayers and I have spotted a few with stun guns. Your only chance is to hide in the bushes and pounce on a newbie (You can tell them by the way they exit their truck. If they keep looking around and load something, better wait).

Once the freezer is opened, we find that, except for a few unruly nomadic cheese sticks and meatballs, the contents have pretty much remained on their respective sides.

After all our procrastination, it only took us a few hours to dig out and break apart all of the packages.

JOHN SIDE

By now, it should not be much of a surprise as to what we discover, but I want to document the event as a lesson to future generations (not sure what the lesson is .... *keep better tabs on the church?*).

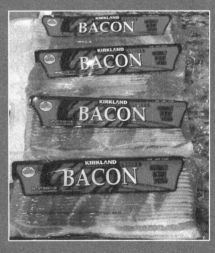

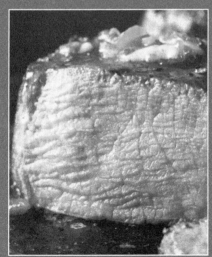

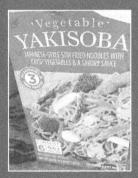

John Total: 175,983 calories

Martha Total: 122 calories

Cheese anyone?

TRAVEL OBSERVATION

Airport April 2020

Airport April 2021

REFINANCE WOES

I am minding my own business outside a small cafe perusing my messages while the lovely Martha is ordering a latte and biscotti.

That is the moment when my phone goes into full blown red alert vibration mode with lights flashing, and whistles blowing.

Lending Tree just announced a 1.75% mortgage rate.

Before you can comprehend the rest of this story, you must know that lower rates to me are like Catnip to cats or a French fry to a starving seagull.

I am on constant alert for an opportunity to re-finance something, *anything*, (the house, our children's wedding receptions, my Shirley Temple tab at Stone Brewery).

Now, I *know* from experience that this is probably a 3-week variable *teaser* rate only available for the next 10 minutes, to newlyweds with a 1000 + FICO score and no priors. This last requirement is always hard for me to overcome. During a mild mid-life crisis, my souped-up Nissan 280 ZX landed me in traffic school more often than a visiting professor at UCLA.

But I digress.

I know better but we're talking 1.75% here. There is only so much a man can take. So, I close my eyes and with the right side of my brain screaming *"DON'T DO IT,"* I do the dreaded deed. I click on *"Learn More."*

It starts out benevolently asking a few basic questions like how much I want to borrow and for how long. From that information and apparently access to the DMV, their algorithm calculates my odds of obtaining this amazing once in a lifetime rate. (I can almost see their computers spitting out transistors and microchips from laughing so hard.)

Sorry Fast Johnny, the best available rate with your driving record, is 15.5% with 7 points.

But wait, apparently all is not lost.

A text appears telling me that if I provide additional information about myself, my relatives, and close friends, who knows what is possible. Go ahead Fast Johnny, just click on that $###$$#### *"Learn More"* button again.

Well, fool me once, ... I try to hang up, but the application won't let me.

I get panicky and frantic; my phone is now possessed. I truly do not know what to do. With every reboot, the loan gods get nastier. I am now being threatened with loan jail if I don't complete an application or squeal on an acquaintance needing money.

Finally, after rebooting 16 times, I am allowed to sign off with a chilling message saying that because of my request, mortgage brokers will be in touch with me to fulfill my refinancing addiction needs.

That is when it dawns on me: ***THEY HAVE MY PHONE NUMBER!***

I might as well destroy my phone. Within an hour I have heard from:

Home Savings, Rocket Mortgage, Wells Fargo, Bank of America, Chase, First American, Last American, Lost American, Found American, Old Republic, New Republic, Middle Age Republic, Citizen Bank, Alien Savings, Veterans United, Disorganized Veterans Fund, Alfredo and Luigi's no questions asked Savings and Loans, Loans "R" us, Flagstar Funding, No Stars Lending, Community Lending, Lone Wolf Bank, etc.......

I know that this is where many of you are thinking, "There he goes, full speed ahead into the *embellishment* zone."

Before you make that judgement, I submit just 2 screen captures out of approximately 700. I have silenced my phone which by now has vibrated itself off my desk and is crawling its way toward an electric socket gasping for some electrons.

It has now been 3 days since "The Incident" and my exhausted, smoking ruin of a phone is barely emitting an audible squeak occasionally. I am, however, down to just a few calls per hour.

But wait, another RED alert?

YES, Lending Twigs just announced a 1.5 % 30-year mortgage for empty nesters with no pets …. *Holy Moly, THAT'S ME!*

Luckily, Martha being near and following my instructions, immediately ties me down with the rope we bought with the cash out from our last refinance.

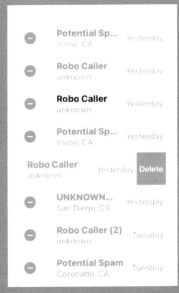

MORE TRAVEL OBSERVATIONS

1. Shower heads are getting higher.

2. Toilet seats are getting lower.

3. Hotel beds are getting so tall, Martha has to stand on my shoulders to "hop in."

4. Within a week of exposure to sun, salt air, and guacamole, your clothes begin shrinking dramatically.

***** I may have found the answer to problem # 3

SHADES OF SHADY PINES

By now, I firmly believe that our children have heard rumors of our latest antics and are getting seriously concerned.

Being banned from a church that we do not even belong to set off a few flares. We tried playing the incidents down. After-all, restraining orders are quite common around Little Italy.

I can tell they are not buying it. I can also tell that they are not quite ready for a full-blown intervention. They have begun circling the subject of the benefits of a retirement community where you don't need big freezers.

Although I cannot prove who the culprits are, yesterday, someone slipped under our door a very suspicious multi page glossy color brochure from the Shady Pines Resort for *"frolicky fun loving seniors."* The brochure depicts a plethora of over-the-top exuberant and joyous elders.

They are riding horses, playing polo (both on horse and in the pool), ziplining, rappelling down the climbing wall, playing flag football, doing the limbo in front of Hawaiian dancers with Tiki torches, going off the high dive holding hands, racing their 10 speed bikes around an indoor track, speeding down a slope in tandem toboggans, playing golf, tennis, basketball and my favorite: sharing a bathtub and drink while watching the sun set in the west. I have to say, with the inclusion of an obvious abundance of drugs, 3 meals per day and free Cha-Cha lessons on Tuesdays, we are almost sold.

But, it's hard to stay ahead of Fast Johnny with his magnifying glass and 30X readers. Way at the bottom of the second page, under a large banner welcoming us to this 24/7 sleepless party haven, I find what I had been looking for: *the fine print* (too small for naked senior eyes.) One paragraph is clearly aimed at easing the mind of relatives and caretakers. It reads: "*At Shady Pines, safety and security are our greatest concern. You will be pleased to know that an escape proof 17-foot barbed wire electrified fence surrounds our Shangri-la. Also, the guards occupying the watch towers (disguised as tall planters) are only permitted to use laughing gas, thin nylon nets and rubber bullets in case of an insurrection. We are proud of our 125-year history of no escapes. Thus, our motto:* **"You can trust us with your loved ones, they're not going anywhere."**

We decided that **_we_** are not ready for Shady Pines, but it did sound like a great place for **_really_** wily seniors. So, in the middle of the night, I drove to my parent's condo and slipped the brochure under **_their_** door.

MEDICAL OBSERVATIONS

I used to go to the doctor regularly, but then, my doctor told me I needed multiple Lumbar fusions.

The next time I went in, he diagnosed me with Parkinson's.

During the following visit, he informed me that I was Pre-Diabetic.

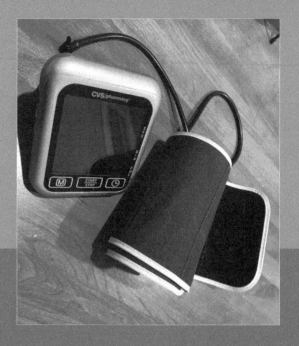

I quit going to the doctor!

Also,

"If you think nobody knows you exist, try missing a couple of car payment" … *Flip Wilson*

"You can't run like a Gazelle if you eat like a horse" … *Fast Johnny*

STELLA'S REVENGE

As I have documented in previous publications, my opinion of men requiring pedicures was rather low. My motto had always been: "Real men don't get pedicures."

That is, until I turned 70 and the balance required to reach my bouncy toes with hand tremors while holding a nail clipper steady became problematic.

That is when I finally caved and succumbed to the Nail Salon experience.

They say you never forget your first. That is so true. I still have recurring nightmares of my first encounter with Stella's Nail Salon.

The COVID lockdown police shut down all salons indefinitely. I dutifully looked chagrined trying to feel Martha's pain and utter panic.

I must confess that not shopping for clothes, no pedicures, no theater Chick Flicks, and not having to go to Cousin Susie's third destination wedding (requiring $1500.00 just in mosquito nets) were thoughts starting to ease my fears of a long and painful lockdown.

Martha and I really did try to give each other acceptable non-destructive pedicures.

After a few valiant efforts, *for the sake of our marriage,* we decided that our only answer was to go to Oregon every few months where rules were laxer, and my sister-in-law had an underground pedicure connection.

We, however, had to stop going there. We were put on the NO-FLY list after getting arrested for joining a group of Portland protesters chanting, "NO *PEDICURES*-NO PEACE."

At the police station, we were informed that the marchers were actually chanting "NO *PROCEDURES* NO PEACE."

An understanding and sympathetic judge, (with uneven jagged toenails sticking out from under a black robe) saved us from the guillotine.

Our punishment was thus limited to being placed on the No-Fly list and a restraining order applicable to all of Oregon.

I could only wear open-toed sandals by the time California allowed salons to reopen (if social distancing was observed and masks were worn).

By then, even I had started looking forward to that day. We called Stella's and were informed that the place was empty, but we should get there fast as they were closing in 15 minutes.

Luckily, we only live 5 minutes away.

We peel rubber to the front door to find the bar scene in the original STAR WARS movie, a chaotic, wall-to-wall mixture of customers, pedicurologists, and nailologists.

Not much social distancing here, but at least everyone was wearing masks. Having been vaccinated and not about to put up with one more day of tripping over our nails and ruining our hard wood floors, we decided to brave it.

I noticed that this close to quitting time, some clients were being double teamed in an effort to close the shop on time.

Across the salon, I spot Stella. Even with my mask on, my hair now down to my shoulders and sporting a cap and sunglasses, I could tell she recognized me. She whispered something in Vietnamese to a co-worker that makes them fall off their tiny stools laughing hysterically. Then she looked back at me. Her look said, "YOU'RE MINE." Oh no, that panicky feeling and instinct to bolt was back.

She sets up a workstation and lays out a plethora of torture devices. I can tell she is grinning under that mask. She then places my feet in what must be a 750-degree lobster boiling foot tub and leaves me to ponder what has become of me.

When she returns, she points at my fingernails mumbling in her mask while shaking her head. Out of nowhere and at the speed of light, a menu appears. Only $40.00 more for cleaning up my fingernail health hazard. I agree that they look pretty bad and why not experience something new.

No sooner have I nodded yes, that Stella 2 grabs a nearby tiny stool and starts cutting my fingernails. Meanwhile, Stella 1 has convinced me that my calluses are in such bad shape that I may require surgery soon. The menu reappears out of nowhere and I tepidly point to "Calluses Extreme."

That immediately triggers Stella 3 to burst out from behind a curtain with an industrial Home Depot size sander (a la Jason) and menacingly head for my workstation.

I had specifically asked for the no-frills basic package, but services have now been bundled. A leg "massage" is included with a pedicure and a manicure includes an arm "massage"? Oh boy, here we go again.

Martha looks over and witnesses Stella 1 pounding on my legs, Stella 2 punching my arms and Stella 3 now wearing noise canceling earphones, sanding away and barely visible in the resulting cloud of dust.

She apparently thinks this is very funny and shares the joke with Stella 4 who is lurking nearby in case I order additional beatings.

One benefit of the power sanding is that it is taking attention away from the leg and arm pain I am enduring because of two Stellas pounding on my limbs. Stella 1, sensing that I am about to bolt, clamps down on my arm with a terminator worthy vice grip. I am not going anywhere.

Coming to that conclusion, I force myself to relax and focus on the giant TV. Luckily, it is showing the same movie as a year ago and I can finally learn what happened to Benji.

Now, I don't want to leave, I must see the end of the movie.

The Stellas are not amused. It is past quitting time.

Squawking like a flock of seagulls, they drag me out of my chair and present me with a $125.00 bill only payable in cash.

I open my wallet and discover that I no longer have that kind of spare change on me.

Of course, Martha is long gone, having settled her measly $45.00 invoice (with the cash she discovered this morning and withdrew from her personal money tree…. my wallet).

The Stellas, once again, fail to see the humor in the situation.

After numerous eye rolls and unintelligible mask obscured comments, I am pointed toward an ATM machine which I know will steal a percentage of my cash.

I dare not bring that up as the murderous looks tell me it is time to go home. I withdraw enough to include a 20% tip.

Now, all smiles, the Stellas unlock the front door and tell me to come back soon. *(At least, I think that's what they said.)* I smile back and walk away thinking that it was not that bad afterall and that the bruises will probably disappear over the next few months.

I also tell myself that the giggles I heard as the door was closing behind me had absolutely nothing to do with me.

REFLECTION

When I was in college, the bulge in my wallet was for well...*hmm*... "protection." Now, it's from my key finder.

I was too honest on the DMV license renewal form and mentioned the dreaded word, *"Parkinson's."*

As a result, I was denied renewal. I must now be interviewed, take a written test, and a supervised road test.

Due to COVID created delays, I now have an outdated license.

During our recent trip to Oregon, two diligent TSA officers pointed that out while contemplating my flying future. Luckily, I was able to convince them that *I* (me)had not expired, just my license.

(Of course, I should probably not have drawn X's over my eyes.)

Meanwhile, my 95-year-old uncle, one county over, who confuses me with my non-existent sister and drives on the left side of the road (because that's how he was taught in the old country), was just renewed for 5 years, no questions asked (*honest to God truth*).

Accepting my fate, I have been pounding the rule book and taking practice tests.

I was whizzing through speed limit questions, what signs meant and how to behave responsibly at stop signs .... easy peazy.

Then I ran into one question that had me baffled. I want to pass it on to you and see if you can answer it.

You are in a car driving towards a steep incline.

You see a fire engine on your right.

You are close to a fence on your left and there is a horse in front of you slowing traffic.

WHAT should you do? **********

Answer at bottom of page.

Also, while perusing the DMV forms needed to fulfill my duties, I ran into this baffler (for real).

"How to renew your lifetime license. Information (916) 928-5805"

*** Put the drink down and get off the carrousel ***

PEPE'S RENEWAL

My father (Pepe), residing in Los Angeles and in his late 80's' with near complete dementia, needed to renew his driver's license. This of course required taking an eye chart test as well as passing the dreaded "rules of the road" written exam.

Did I mention his dementia?

Based on a few recent hair-raising tales of his daily outings roaming the streets of LA, I welcomed the test. It was going to achieve something I had not been able to accomplish. His failing the test would finally allow me to justifiably TAKE HIS CAR KEYS AWAY!!

So, with much enthusiasm, I drove down to LA with a foolproof plan. I hoped to convince my mother (whose life was in daily danger) that we should avoid the embarrassing disaster about to happen if my father showed up at the DMV. My suggestion was to not even bother with the test and just tell him he flunked it the week before.

Ah, naïve *Fast Johnny* …. still believing after all these years that he could manipulate his parents with logic.

Somehow, my fiery Italian mother (with a verified 6th sense) had deduced my dastardly plot.

As soon as I turned into their driveway, I knew my plan was already unraveling. There she was, waiting for me outside with arms crossed and full Italian pout. Before I could even open my door, she announced that:

"Pepe is going to keep driving, period, end of story!!!"

He was just as stubborn, not realizing of course that he had a few driving issues (*like knowing where the hell he was*).

The thought of him remaining loose on the streets of LA was truly terrifying.

Miraculously, with him at the wheel (usually totally lost), and my mother navigating by instinct and a Ouija Board, they always managed to get home without killing themselves or mowing down any innocent bystanders.

I still marvel to this day at this logic defying feat.

But I digress. As a compromise, I offered to take him to take the test.

Fast Johnny, as sharp as ever, predicted that he would fail and that would be the end of it. *Ha, ha, ha, poor Johnny, so fast yet so slow.*

At that time, there were only 10 tests

given to Southern California license applicants. *Yes, the same tests* for long periods of time.

The Italian community had discovered this fact, had acquired all the tests over time and ran an underground DMV test library.

If you memorized the first answer of the 10 tests, you would know which test you were dealing with at the DMV. Since you also memorized the order of the answers on each test, easy peazy (even if you did not know English).

Well, of course, my determined mother had been drilling him for weeks, using these tests.

I was not worried one bit, smugly knowing that he could never pass, I mean the man could not remember where his bedroom was.

We are now about to leave for the DMV office, and I notice that he was not wearing his glasses.

OK, this is a man that has a drawer containing at least 30 pairs of glasses.

For those of you old enough, think of Red Foxx's eyeglass drawer in the TV series "SANFORD AND SON" …. not kidding.

When questioned, he tells me that his eyesight has improved tremendously over the past year and that he does not need glasses anymore.

This surprised me because at the breakfast table, he was reading the paper with the print only about an inch from his face.

He also claimed that at his last eye exam, he was told that he had a severe cataract and needed surgery.

His conclusion (since he now had perfect vision) was that the doctor was a total quack and a crook trying to fleece him of his meager pension. He, furthermore, was never seeing another eye doctor **EVER!**

Of course, arguing with my Dad had been pointless my entire life. Therefore, to avoid one of his famous tirades, I simply agreed that everyone except members of our immediate family were crooks, on the take, and after our money. Mind you, not the entire immediate family. He has never trusted Uncle Minouchi *(always with the f######## camera documenting)*.

I gave up on the glasses and we headed for the DMV office.

On the way, I decided to test this new theory of perfect vision.

I spotted a large distant sign for the 405 freeway and nonchalantly asked him if he could see the freeway sign.

He may have had dementia, but the old goat is immediately onto me. He sarcastically answers "Of course Sonny Boy, what do you think? I have perfect vision."

OK, I am impressed, but unconvinced. I try again with a smaller sign.

Again, the same result but with a bit more irritation in his voice.

Wow, maybe his eyesight *is* better.

Then it dawns on me, and I am reluctant to ask the obvious: "Uh, Dad, could you *read* what the signs said?"

To which he answers quite irritated, "Are you out of your *F%%%$$#g* mind, what am I, a *F##%%#g* hawk? I told you, I can see the sign, it's blurry but I can see it."

Trying to determine the level of this perfect vision, and once he has calmed down, I ask: "Can you tell me when you are able to read the approaching large green sign?" As we are literally rolling under the sign, he blurts out, "Pasadena 20 miles ......see, perfect vision."

Correct answer but it's timing tells me that this man has the vision of a desert mole. No way is he passing the vision test.

We arrive at the testing center, and he admires the architecture of the building.

He, of course, flunks both the eye test and written portion in spectacular fashion. He has already forgotten what we are doing and is very upset at me for taking him to another eye care center .... and again, with the *F$$$$G* eye chart.

He hands me his test which he thinks is a prescription. I see that he had drawn test #8. Rats, he had done so much better on #3 at home.

The clerk informs us that he gets three attempts to pass the test. We can either come back another day or try again in one hour.

I decide not to prolong this ordeal and agree to come back in one hour for another exam.

This gave us enough time to get a cup of coffee at a nearby café.

There, I searched the car for a pair of glasses. I found one in the trunk under his emergency and self-defense arsenal (a crowbar, a baseball bat, a can of mace, two box cutters, and a few stray bullets from a gun he has not seen in 25 years).

Confident that we can defend ourselves from any imminent threat, we return to the scene of the crime. In the immortal words of Yogi Berra *"It's Deja-vu all over again."*

He sees the building and once again admires the architecture having no recollection of just being there.

He then asks me what we are doing here and that it better not be to see a *G## ###N* eye doctor. I promise him that we are not going to the eye doctor.

Of course, as soon as we walk in, he spots the eye charts behind the workers. It takes all of my strength to keep him from bolting. His look is one of panic mixed with a touch of *"YOU SOB, how could you, you traitor."*

I again calm him down. Donning his slightly bent, scratched and dirty newfound glasses, he passes the eye test.

Unfortunately (or fortunately), he draws test #9, but to my amazement only fails the test by two questions.

I call my mother to inform her that we have only one more chance and that I am convinced more than ever to give up on this Don Quixote effort.

We must take his keys away!!!

Meanwhile, she has buried a small statue of St. Joseph upside down in the yard. Italians do this to expedite the sale of property. She figures that if this works for real estate, it just might work for a driver's license. *Fast Gina*, leaving no stone unturned.

She orders me, her worthless son, to bring him home where she will take over again and double her efforts.

She could not believe that I had not found a way to help him. She bets I ignored her advice again and did not have the guts to flash some green at the testing clerk (like in the old days). She storms out of the house and buries another statue.

I make the near fatal mistake of expressing doubt about the effectiveness of the statues. This triggers an Italian/French/English word soup tirade. It ends with her reminding me (for the 12 millionth time) that if she only had had a daughter, she would not have all these F########g problems.

I decided that my help was no longer needed (or wanted) and headed back to San Jose, the land of the sane.

One week later, my mother calls me and in her best "Neener-Neener" voice proudly announces that she took my dad back to the DMV and he passed test #3 with only one mistake. She had been drilling him 24/7 since I left, buried 7 more statues, and he lucked out getting the desired test.

She was also convinced that the 12-pound box of Sees Candy and a small suitcase of chocolate chip cookies that she spread around the DMV office put it over the top.

The statues were back on the mantle and the holes filled in (although the yard looked like it was invaded by a herd of crazed gophers).

All was well again in the world, and they were fully authorized by the state of California to roam the streets of the metropolis freely for another 5 years.

So it came to pass that they continued terrorizing their neighborhood and our family for a few more years.

We eventually moved them to San Diego where I was finally able to convince them that it was time to give up the keys.

JOHN'S DRIVING TEST

I am pleased to announce that I have been cleared to terrorize neighborhoods again.

After being thoroughly penalized for telling the truth (about Parkinson's) and a 7-month quest to get my license renewed, I passed the driving test today.

This was the last step, and it was a doozy. I should have known right away when I was pulled out of the lineup of teen age test takers.

The officer looked at me and said "Ah, you must be our **"SPECIAL CASE"**.

OK, What the hell does that mean? Shades of Stella panic attacks are back.

What it meant was a 40-minute test instead of the standard 10-20 minutes.

We went through construction zones dodging cones and open pits.

We went through a homeless area dodging meandering citizens and shopping carts.

Then, we got on the dreaded Highway 163.

My dilemma was to keep up with traffic going about 80 mph or obey the speed limit of 55mph.

I kind of split the baby at 65mph.

Wrong decision. My panicked passenger is now yelling at me to step on it and keep up with the traffic or we might get killed.

We thus go *careening* towards downtown San Diego with the exit to the Mexican border getting too near for my comfort.

At the last minute, still going 80mph (to test my reflexes I suppose), he yells " take the next exit, **now**!" …. which I do on two wheels, I think.

What follows is a very pleasant ride through Balboa Park, then, by Ruben's and the Zoo.

We finally got back to the testing center, and I was sure that I had flunked.

I mean, the man never stopped twitching or writing on his clipboard.

To my amazement, he says **"That was some fine driving young man, you passed with flying colors".** I was only deducted 4 points out of an allowed 30."

Of course, I will never know if he passed me due to my superb careening skills or the fear of my return for another try.

PASTA MANIA UPDATE

As of the writing of "Lockdown Capers," I was all in with the making my own pasta get-rich-quick scheme. As you may recall, I only needed to make 172 pounds of assorted pasta to break even (if someone donated the ricotta and VONS drastically increased their pasta prices).

Unfortunately, neither of these things have happened. I am still waiting for a ricotta donor and pasta futures have plunged due to the increased competition from zucchini and flourless based products. I googled "non flour pastas" and to my dismay, found these top selling tasty treats:

1. Shirataki **Noodles** ·

2. **Spaghetti** Squash ·

3. Cricket **Pasta** ·

4. Kelp **Noodles** ·

5. Zoodles ·

6. Cellophane **Noodles** ·

7. Chickpea **Pasta**.

These gelatinous Japanese noodles are made from the Konjac yam plant.

Yum Yum, Cricket Pasta!

In addition to these market forces, I am facing an increasingly skeptical Martha. The first 25 pounds of flour are gone. But, I have zero revenue to report. She is also very suspicious that my weight gain may not strictly be due to COVID anxiety as I have been claiming.

So, what to do?

The only logical thing, ***DOUBLE DOWN!!!!***

I decided to fight fire with fire (or in this case, vegetables with glutens). I needed to expand my product line as well as improve the efficiency of my production.

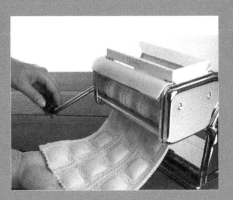

This, however, only increased my market vertically. I needed to expand horizontally by adding products besides pastas.

Making ravioli one at a time was a real time-consuming beast. So, I bought a new more automated attachment ($70.00).

Then I discovered and bought a plethora of attachments that I needed for my expansion ($250.00).

I am proud to announce that in addition to my "express" ravioli, I can now make all the pictured pastas.

No seaweed in these puppies!

The answer, of course, is a portable pizza oven ($450.00).

Redoing the math yields a new investment total of $986.00.

It also yields a new breakeven point well into the next century.

Good thing Martha likes pizza!!

PILL MAGIC UPDATE

As you will recall from Lockdown Capers, so many of our pills were ending up under the refrigerator, that we use it as our emergency backup pharmacy.

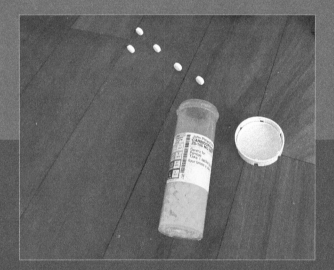

Well, you do have to take inventory occasionally.

LIGHTS UPDATE

After wandering around the house in the dark for months, We are announcing that thanks to our window washer's help, the house is once again bathed in golden light.

GLASSES AND AMAZON UPDATE

Reading Glasses Update

Those of you who read "Lockdown Capers" will recall my frustrating inability to keep track of my readers. Well, fret no more mi amigos. Thanks to the bulk department at Amazon and a new wall rack, the problem is solved … well, except for Martha who would apparently rather have me crashing into walls than admit that my new wall décor is not that bad.

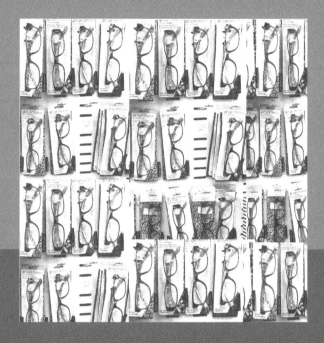

Amazon Update

We remain the number one Amazon customers. How do you think Jeff could afford the gas for that space joy ride? Overwhelmed with boxes, we held a recycling break down party.

***** BULLETIN***we got the Amazon credit card which rebates 5% on every purchase. we save enough each month to cover one of our car payments.

SMART APPLIANCES AND WATCH UPDATE

Smart Appliances Update

We have begun a counterattack against our smart appliances. We decided, for example, that we did not need to look at our oven to tell time. Or use it to set an alarm to tell us when the tea is done. (Did you know they made pots that whistle when the tea is ready?)

So, we replaced our oven with a lovely, not internet and network connected stove.

We have not heard a peep from any of our kitchen gismos since. They are either terrified or planning a coup. Alexa has been creepy quiet, and we only hear her talk when we are upstairs.

When we do address her with a question, I suspect that she is giving us wrong answers. I tested that theory this morning by asking what city the capital of France was. She answered Rome. OK, she got that one right, but I am still suspicious.

Smart Watch Update

I was fed up with my constantly whining smart sports watch. We were obviously not compatible. We tried to make it work. We even went to the Apple store and signed up for counseling services. We were amazed at the size of the support groups in attendance. This is obviously a very common problem. Unfortunately, during one of the sessions, a beautiful and younger model caught my eye. In addition to her beauty, she was the Sloth model that I had been lusting after since Apple announced that it featured a GPS unit that not only told you how to get to your destination but told you why you wanted to go there in the first place. During a break, she cozied up to me and whispered the magic words, "Take me home and you will never have to exercise again." Readers, meet my new trophy watch **Slothy Belle.**

THE FINAL WORD

So, the more things change, the more they stay the same. Now, as this book is going to print, a new strain has taken hold and is devastating parts of the country. We are advised to get a booster shot but once again, the rules and regulations are all over the map. We go to our local CVS and the staff is indifferent. "You want a booster, sure why not, are you positive you are older than twelve?". One nurse checks our temperature and Martha is informed that her temperature is too high, and we will have to come back. Oh Lord, here we go again.

John R. Pistacchi

After 30 years running a successful Silicon Valley computer services firm, John Pistacchi, and his partner in Crime (spouse) Martha, sold the business and retired to San Diego. This is when John returned to an old hobby, publishing. His first endeavors involved freelance articles for Reader's Digest and the American Airline's in-flight magazine. During this time, John also published a video series on fishing various areas of California. The COVID lockdown gave John the time to get serious and put his wicked sense of humor to broader use. This endeavor resulted in the successful launch of his first book *Lockdown Capers* chronicling John and Martha's hilarious adaptation to evolving lockdown related circumstances. The book at one point reached the top 100 best sellers on Amazon in the category of marriage humor. This encouraged John to write a sequel covering the period immediately following the lockdown.

OTHER BOOKS BY JOHN R. PISTACCHI

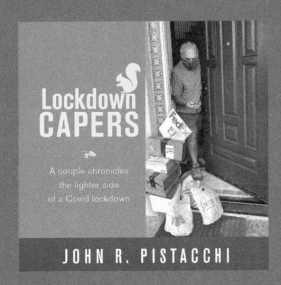

LOCKDOWN CAPERS

NATURE TALKS (Volume 1)

As mentioned previously, John published his first book *Lockdown Capers* in early 2021. The book chronicles the humorous side of a couple facing being together 24/7 as a complete lockdown takes effect in California.

The result is a funny romp through their dealing with protocols, masks, hoarding, and shortages of toilet paper and flour.

For years, John has been entertaining his grandchildren and their friends with postcards. These feature his (and their) photography and talking animals, plants, and nature in general. They have been so popular and entertaining that John consolidated their favorites into a children's book available on Amazon.

Photograph by Zack Peck Age 11

CPSIA information can be obtained
at www.ICGtesting.com
Printed in the USA
LVHW070836150122
708351LV00004B/49